William Shakespeare

THE INSPRING LIFE STORY OF THE PLAYWRIGHT EXTRAORDINAIRE

BY PAMELA HILL NETTLETON

COMPASS POINT BOOKS
a capstone imprint

Compass Point Books are published by Capstone,
1710 Roe Crest Drive, North Mankato, Minnesota 56003
www.mycapstone.com

Copyright © 2017 by Compass Point Books, a Capstone imprint.
All rights reserved. No part of this publication may be reproduced in whole
or in part, or stored in a retrieval system, or transmitted in any form or by
any means, electronic, mechanical, photocopying, recording, or otherwise,
without written permission of the publisher.

Editorial Credits
Catherine Neitge and Angela Kaelberer, editors; Ashlee Suker, designer;
Wanda Winch, media researcher; Kathy McColley, production specialist

Photo Credits
AP Images: Press Association/Shakespeare's Globe/PA Wire URN:5157312, 27; Art Resource, NY: V&A Images, London, 68, foto Marburg, 76, HIP, 6, The Philadelphia Museum of Art, 96; Bridgeman Images: G. Nimatallah/De Agostini Picture Library/Annibale Carracci, 33, Index, Barcelona/Biblioteca de Catalunya, Barcelona, Spain/William Morris, 59, 103, Private Collection/English School, 41, The Maas Gallery, London/Private Collection/Eleanor Fortescue-Brickdale, 13; Capstone, 10, 84; Dreamstime: Davidmartyn, 101; Getty Images: Archive Photos, 56, Corbis/Dean Conger, 92, Hulton Archive, 8, 54, 72, Imagno, 82, Print Collector, 71, Rischgitz, 48, Stock Montage, 88, The LIFE Images Collection/Mansell/Time Life Pictures, 4, 80, The LIFE Images Collection/Sahm Doherty, 98; Granger, NYC – All rights reserved, 28, 37, 44, 102; Mary Evans Picture Library, 14, 21, 66; Newscom: Design Pics, 61, EPA/Justin Lane, 95, Heritage Images/Fine Art Images, 29; The National Archives of the UK [By Me William Shakespeare Exhibit – Shakespeare's Will, sheet 3], 91; North Wind Picture Archives, 63, 104; Shutterstock: Claudio Divizia, 22, Everett Historical, 23, Markovka, feather design element, Morag Fleming, 34, PHB.cz (Richard Semik), 86, 105; SuperStock: Pantheon/Mar/Illustrated London News Ltd, 75, SuperStock, 53, 78; Thinkstock: Photos.com, 24

Library of Congress Cataloging-in-Publication Data
Names: Nettleton, Pamela Hill, author.
Title: William Shakespeare : the inspiring life story of the playwright extraordinaire / By Pamela Hill Nettleton.
Description: North Mankato, Minnesota : Compass Point Books, an imprint of Capstone Press, 2017. | Series: CPB grades 4-8. Inspiring stories | Includes bibliographical references and index.
Identifiers: LCCN 2016004348
ISBN 9780756551636 (library binding)
ISBN 9780756551858 (ebook pdf)
Subjects: LCSH: Shakespeare, William, 1564-1616—Juvenile literature. | Authors, English—Early modern, 1500-1700—Biography—Juvenile literature. | Dramatists, English—Early modern, 1500-1700—Biography—Juvenile literature.
Classification: LCC PR2894 .N45 2017 | DDC 822.3/3 [B]—dc23
LC record available at http://lccn.loc.gov/2016004348

Printed and bound in Canada.
009644F16

Table of Contents

CHAPTER ONE
THE WORLD'S BEST 5

CHAPTER TWO
EARLY YEARS 15

CHAPTER THREE
SCHOOLING AND BEYOND 25

CHAPTER FOUR
MARRIAGE AND FAMILY 35

CHAPTER FIVE
EARLY SUCCESS IN LONDON 45

CHAPTER SIX
A PUBLISHED POET 57

CHAPTER SEVEN
SUCCESS AS A PLAYWRIGHT 67

CHAPTER EIGHT
ACHIEVING FAME 79

CHAPTER NINE
LATER YEARS 89

TIMELINE 102
GLOSSARY 106
ADDITIONAL RESOURCES 107
SOURCE NOTES 108
SELECT BIBLIOGRAPHY 110
INDEX 111
CRITICAL THINKING USING THE COMMON CORE 112

William Shakespeare is considered the greatest writer of all time.

Chapter One
THE WORLD'S BEST

It was September 7, 1592, in the bustling, crowded city of London, England. A 28-year-old actor and playwright named William Shakespeare had just heard some very bad news. The theater where he acted and produced his plays had just closed. And he couldn't find a job at another theater—all the theaters in London were ordered closed. Why? A horrible disease called the bubonic plague was killing people.

The plague had been sweeping periodically through Europe since the mid-1300s. People who became sick with the plague experienced fever,

Inspiring Stories

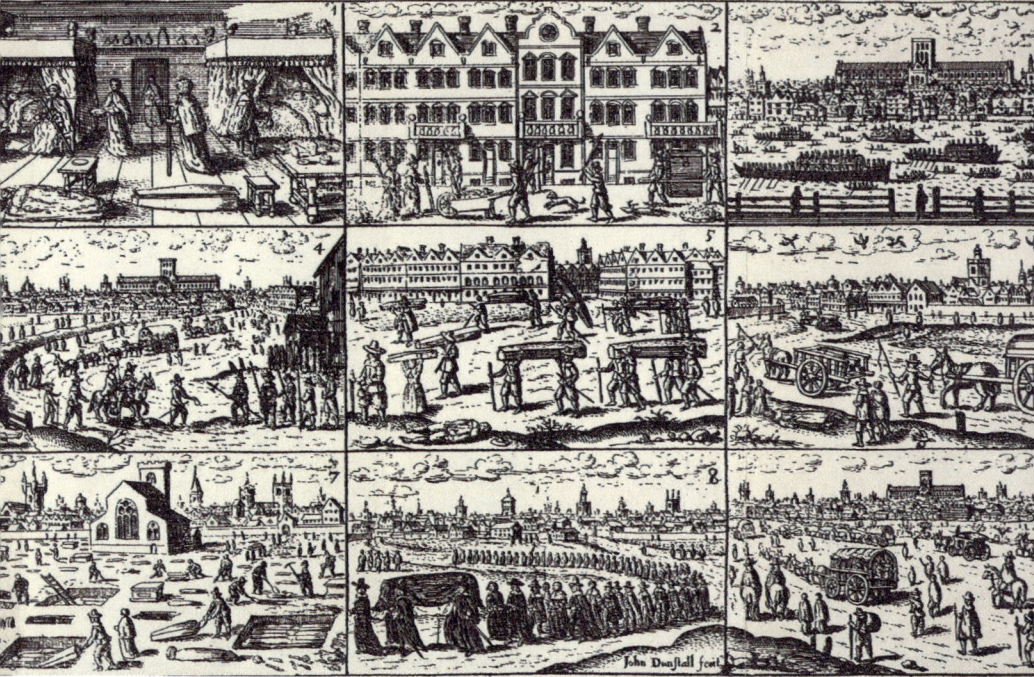

An engraving features the various stages of the plague as it devastates a town.

chills, and black bumps under the arms and on the sides of the neck. These painful bumps were called buboes and gave the bubonic plague its name. Almost everyone who had the plague died, and it was so contagious that most of that person's family and friends would become infected and die as well.

At the time no one knew what caused the plague. Today we know that fleas living on the rats that roamed the streets and houses of every European city carried

THE PLAGUE

Europeans lived in fear of the bubonic plague for hundreds of years. Entire towns and villages perished all at once from the terrible disease. During the year 1625 alone, the plague killed one-fifth of England's population.

So many people died at once that men drove wagons down the streets collecting bodies. "Bring out your dead," they would shout. Families would carry out anyone who had died during the night. Bodies were buried in mass graves.

The plague eventually ended when brown rats took over the places where black rats ate and lived. Plague-carrying fleas didn't live on the brown rats, so as brown rats became dominant, the plague lost its grip on Europe.

Bubonic plague and the other types of plague are rare today, but cases still crop up from time to time, especially in poorer countries. The disease is now treatable with antibiotics.

Inspiring Stories

A Midsummer Night's Dream *is one of Shakespeare's most famous plays.*

the disease. But people understood that the plague was contagious and wanted to limit gatherings of large numbers of people in close quarters. The theaters were ordered closed and wouldn't open until the plague ran its course, about two years later.

Shakespeare wasn't sure what he was going to do. He had been in London for several years and was finally earning a decent living for himself and his family, who lived in the small town of Stratford about 75 miles (120 kilometers) northwest of London. People who weren't able to work often starved to death. Shakespeare was going to have to find some other way to earn money. But how?

Today many people consider William Shakespeare the world's greatest playwright. During a period of about 20 years, he's believed to have written 37 plays and 159 poems. Even more amazing, all of his plays are read, studied, and performed today—400 years after his death. The greatest actors of today find Shakespearean roles the most demanding and difficult to play, yet

Inspiring Stories

Shakespeare spent his entire life in England, probably living only in two towns—Stratford and London.

Shakespeare wrote his plays to entertain the common people of London.

Not many things are known for certain about William Shakespeare's life because people kept few records. His plays, however, show us that Shakespeare was a keen observer of both people and the life of his time. Centuries before there were such things as therapists and counselors, Shakespeare understood people. Shakespeare watched how people behaved and how they treated each other, and he considered the reasons behind their behavior. His characters seem very real because he based them on what he knew about the people in his life.

SHAKESPEARE'S LANGUAGE

Shakespeare's plays were written in Old English, which takes some effort for modern ears to understand. But once that happens, people today hear the truth in his words. Shakespeare's language and phrasing expresses feelings all people have but sometimes have trouble putting into words.

Inspiring Stories

Many playwrights specialize in one type of play. But Shakespeare's plays encompassed comedies, tragedies, and histories of England's kings and wars. He translated everyday life, as well as the stories of kings and queens, into plays everyone could relate to. As he wrote in one of his plays, *As You Like It*, "All the world's a stage, and all the men and women merely players."

Many historians believe that much of Shakespeare's work was based on events from his own life. When he wrote about young love in plays such as *Romeo and Juliet*, he may well have been writing about how he felt as a young man courting his future wife. Perhaps the reason audiences feel so strongly for Hamlet after the loss of his father was that Shakespeare was writing about his grief after the death of his young son. He also must have had a good sense of humor, because even his most tragic plays often have moments that make audiences laugh.

William Shakespeare

Romeo and Juliet part in a scene from one of Shakespeare's most popular plays.

Shakespeare grew up in the town of Stratford, England, which is on the river Avon.

Chapter Two
EARLY YEARS

Not much is known for sure about William Shakespeare's life, especially his early years. In England during Shakespeare's time, few written records were kept, aside from church records. All that was recorded for many people were their dates of baptism, marriage, and burial. For that reason, we don't know for certain the date of Shakespeare's birth. Church records show he was baptized April 26, 1564, at Holy Trinity Church in Stratford, England. That means he was likely born in April, perhaps just a few days before his baptism. According to the custom at that time,

Inspiring Stories

LACK OF LITERACY

Shakespeare's plays are full of irony, as was his life. The playwright was one of the greatest writers of all time, for example, but he had parents who couldn't read or write.

William's mother, Mary Arden, was a farmer's daughter, but she was related to a family of high social standing in the area. Her lack of literacy wasn't unusual for the time. Very few women could read or write, and none attended school. If a girl could read, it was because her father or brother taught her at home. William's sister Joan could sign her name, so William or one of his younger brothers must have taught her.

William's father, John, grew up on a farm and never attended school either. Even after he became mayor of Stratford, John signed his name with a mark.

babies were baptized at about three days of age. Most historians accept a Shakespeare birthdate of April 23, 1564.

William's parents were John Shakespeare and Mary Arden Shakespeare. They married in about 1557. John was a craftsman who made gloves, aprons, and other items out of leather. He also sold wool and may have sold farm products. He wasn't rich, but he was respected in Stratford. He served for many years on the town council and eventually was elected mayor. Although he served for only one term, he remained a town leader for many years. Mary's father was Robert Arden, a successful farmer and landowner. When people married at that time, the bride often brought a dowry—land and money from her father that became the property of the newly married couple. Mary's large dowry of money and land added to John's status in Stratford.

William was the third of eight children, but he was the oldest child to survive childhood. At the time there were no hospitals or good medical care, so many babies didn't live long after birth. Illnesses were especially common among children, and it was typical that a family would lose at least one child to illness at a very young age. Many children didn't live past the age of 5, partly because modern vaccines didn't exist. William's two older sisters both died as babies, and his younger sister Anne died at age 7. But his three younger brothers—Gilbert, Richard, and Edmund—and one younger sister, Joan, lived to adulthood. William was lucky to live himself. When he was less than 3 months old, the bubonic plague came to Stratford. One of the Shakespeares' neighbors lost all four children to the disease. But the Shakespeare family managed to escape the plague.

The Shakespeare family lived on Henley Street in Stratford, a small town in a part of England called Warwickshire. Because the town is located on the river Avon, it is sometimes called Stratford-Upon-Avon or Stratford-on-Avon.

English society at that time had a strict class system. Children were born into whatever class their parents

STRONG WOMEN

Some historians believe that Shakespeare must have been close to his mother and sisters, because female characters in his plays are generally shown in a favorable light. This is especially interesting because women weren't allowed to play a major role in society at the time outside of caring for their homes and families.

Other playwrights and authors often created female characters that were weak or frail. But Shakespeare's women are typically independent, strong-willed, and confident. Even when his female characters do bad or mischievous things, the audience generally understands why and has a positive feeling about the character.

Inspiring Stories

belonged. Royalty or nobles, such as lords and ladies, were in the highest class. Peasants, the poor, and the uneducated made up the lower classes. In between were people like the Shakespeare family.

Before his marriage, it appears that John Shakespeare had some success in business, since he had bought two additional homes in Stratford. As John's business became more successful, he did something he hoped would advance his family's social class. In 1569 he applied to the College of Arms asking for a coat of arms.

A coat of arms is a design made for just one family. The design often looks like a shield or a banner and contains symbols that represent the family. If the family raised sheep and lived in the hills, for example, their coat of arms might include a sheep and a hillside. The coat of arms was used on doors, clothing, flags, and household goods. If a family had a coat of arms, it meant they were of a higher class.

But the College of Arms denied John's request. No one knows exactly why. William was only 5 years old

William Shakespeare

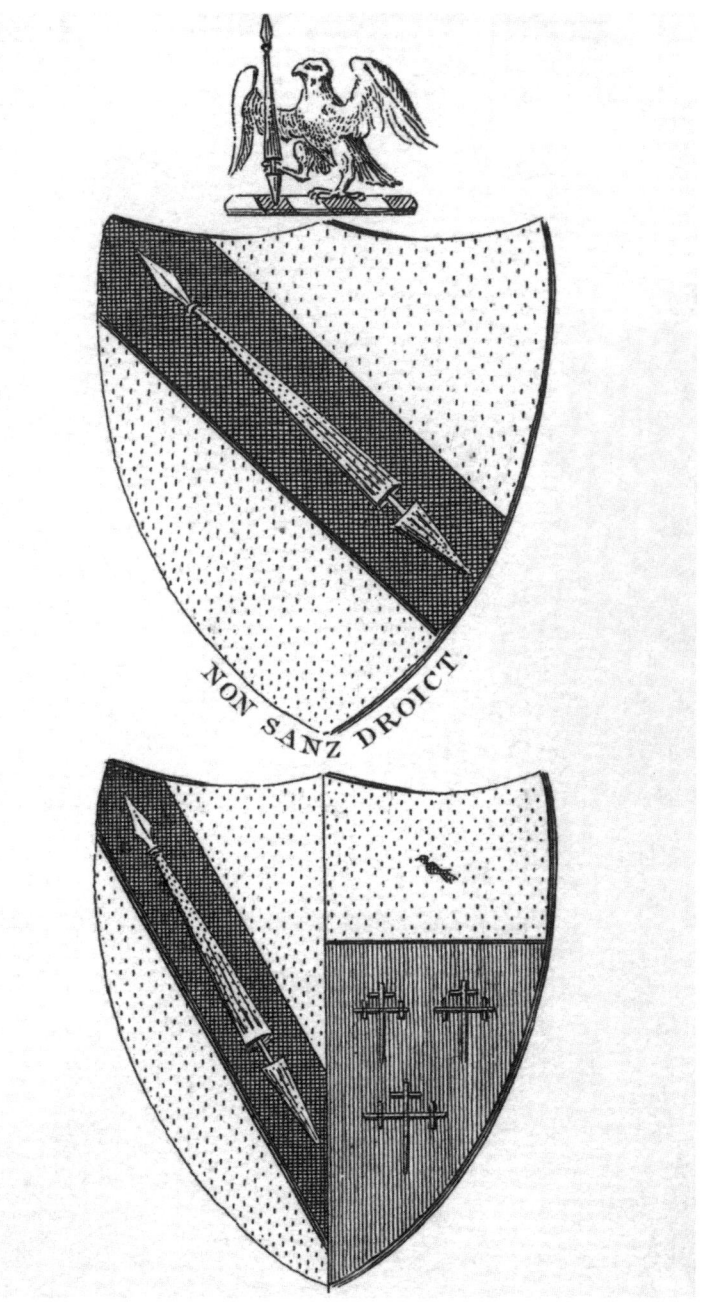

Shakespeare would eventually receive a coat of arms in 1596.

Inspiring Stories

Shakespeare's birthplace draws many visitors to Stratford.

at the time, but apparently his father's desire for a coat of arms was something that he paid attention to. Years later when he became successful, he would apply for a Shakespeare coat of arms—a request that was granted.

Life at a Glance

DATE OF BIRTH:	Unknown; probably April 23, 1564
BIRTHPLACE:	Stratford, England
FATHER:	John Shakespeare
MOTHER:	Mary Arden Shakespeare
EDUCATION:	Grammar school
SPOUSE:	Anne Hathaway (1556–1623)
DATE OF MARRIAGE:	1582
CHILDREN:	Susanna (1583–1649) Judith (1585–1662) Hamnet (1585–1596)
DATE OF DEATH:	April 23, 1616
PLACE OF BURIAL:	Holy Trinity Church, Stratford, England

Elizabeth I began her 45-year reign as queen of England six years before Shakespeare's birth.

Chapter Three
SCHOOLING AND BEYOND

No one knows for sure where William Shakespeare attended school. At that time schools seldom kept written records of their pupils. But historians believe that William probably began school when he was about 7 at the King's New School near his home in Stratford. Like all schools at the time, the King's New School was for boys only.

William spent a lot of time in school. Students met six days a week, and there were no breaks for holidays or vacations. Classes started at 6:00 a.m. and continued until students went home for dinner at about 6:00 p.m. Teachers were strict, and students were physically punished if they broke the rules. The boys learned to read, write, add, and subtract. They also studied Latin. The ability to read and understand Latin, the language of ancient Rome, was a sign of an educated person. Anyone who wanted to be a doctor, lawyer, or priest also needed a good knowledge of Latin.

After three years in grammar school, William moved on to the upper school. He probably read the works of ancient Roman writers such as the philosopher Cicero and the poets Virgil and Ovid. William's love of the classic Latin writings shows up in many of the plots of his plays. Ovid's epic poem the *Metamorphoses* especially had an effect on Shakespeare's work, as seen in one of his early poems, *Venus and Adonis*.

Shakespeare's education wasn't advanced, but he did receive basic rhetorical training. He learned to consider all sides of a situation in order to be able to make a fair and impartial judgment. The training shows through in much of Shakespeare's work. He was able to show each

William Shakespeare

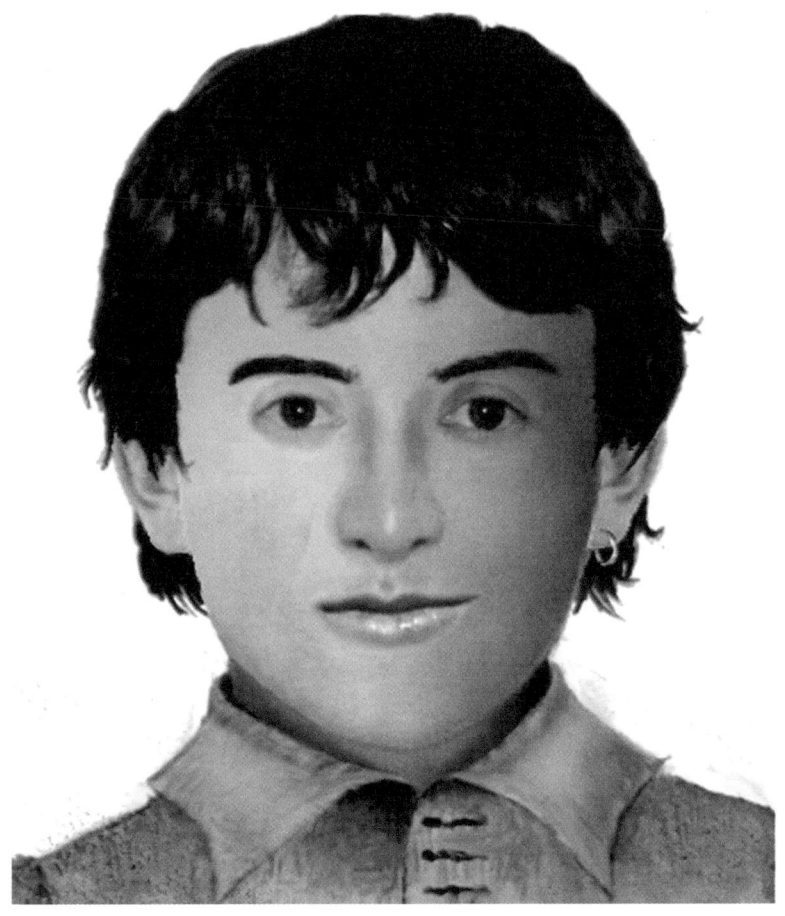

A recent drawing indicates what Shakespeare may have looked like at age 14.

character's point of view to the audience. It allowed the audience to understand why characters acted in certain ways. Like people in real life, none of Shakespeare's characters was all good or all bad.

Inspiring Stories

Shakespeare probably attended the King's New School in Stratford.

Religious studies were also an important part of education. The Shakespeare family belonged to the official state church, the Church of England, also known as the Anglican Church. At school William memorized Anglican prayers, lessons, and psalms. At church he attended catechism classes and studied the Bible. Some Bible themes and stories are even

SHAKESPEARE AND RELIGION

Queen Elizabeth I was an Anglican and the head of the Church of England. Her father, King Henry VIII, established the church in the 1530s when the pope, the head of the Roman Catholic Church, wouldn't allow him to divorce his first wife. Though there is some evidence that Shakespeare's father was a Roman Catholic or had Catholic leanings, the family kept it secret, probably because of persecution and prejudice against Catholics. Publicly the Shakespeare family belonged to the Church of England.

referenced in his plays. Most literate people of Shakespeare's time were familiar with the Bible, so using its stories as a framework for plays was another way to reach his audience.

William probably didn't attend school for more than a few years. By the time he was about 13, his father's business was struggling, and the family was having trouble paying its bills. John was a kindhearted man who went out of his way to help others, sometimes at his own expense. He often agreed to stand surety for friends' loans, for example. It meant that if the borrower couldn't or wouldn't repay the loan, John was responsible for the money. He also posted bail for friends who were charged with crimes. If the friends didn't show up for their court dates, John didn't get his bail money back. He sold some of his property to raise money, but his debts were piling up.

The family's money issues probably had a great effect on William. Years later he included this famous line in his play *Hamlet*, "Neither a borrower nor a lender be."

A DIFFERENT TIME

Life during Shakespeare's time was very different from today. There was no electricity, indoor plumbing, or other modern conveniences. Women hauled water from wells. They cooked meals over fires in big fireplaces. Men farmed or worked at such trades as candle making or printing. Houses were small.

Because there was no running water, homes and restaurants, which were called taverns, were often dirty. There were no refrigerators to keep food from spoiling. People seldom took baths or washed their clothes, so they smelled bad and sometimes had fleas or lice living on them. Since there was no indoor plumbing, human waste was often thrown into the streets or the rivers. The unsanitary conditions allowed germs to multiply and diseases to spread. People often died from eating spoiled food or from contagious diseases. Medical treatment was poor. Often the only treatment a doctor could offer was to cut open a person's vein to release blood. Being "bled" was believed to rid the body of germs and toxins. Instead, it weakened people who were already sick, and they usually became sicker or died as a result of the bleeding. Average life expectancy was 42 years, compared to 78 years in the United States today.

But even with all the problems, Shakespeare's time was considered a period of great progress and growth. He was born during the reign of Queen Elizabeth I. The Elizabethan Era lasted from 1558 to 1603 and included many advances in art and science. People in Europe were expanding their knowledge of the world by exploring the land, the sea, and even the heavens.

Inspiring Stories

William's parents couldn't afford to continue to send him to school, let alone to college. But many boys of William's social class left school at 12 or 13 to learn a trade as an apprentice to a master craftsman. An apprentice left home to live and work with a craftsman for several years. They usually weren't paid, but did receive room, board, and training. It's possible that William apprenticed with his father or some other craftsman, although there's no record that it ever happened.

No one knows exactly what William did between his birth and when he reached age 18. But the plays he wrote years later provide some clues. Shakespeare appeared to have a great deal of knowledge about the law, for example. He may have worked as a clerk in a lawyer's office. In several plays he writes about butchering, so he may have helped slaughter animals or tan hides.

He might also have worked for a time as a tutor for the children of a wealthy family. If so, he may have seen plays performed in the house's great hall by

Shakespeare possibly worked as a butcher as a young man.

traveling troupes of actors. It might have been his first exposure to acting and stage plays. The performances might have inspired him to consider going to London to become an actor or even a playwright. But again, there is no proof of what really happened—until 1582.

Anne Hathaway lived in a cottage in Shottery, England, before her marriage to Shakespeare.

Chapter Four
MARRIAGE AND FAMILY

The next thing we know for certain about William Shakespeare happened in 1582. On November 28 he applied for and received a marriage license. His bride was Anne Hathaway, the daughter of a farmer from the nearby village of Shottery. William was 18 years old, and Anne was 26.

Anne's father, Richard Hathaway, was a friend of John Shakespeare, who had guaranteed a debt for Richard in 1566. Richard's first wife, Anne's mother, had died, and he had since remarried. Richard died in September 1581, leaving Anne a dowry of money but no property.

There's no record of how Anne and William met. After her father's death, Anne may have left her stepmother's home to live with relatives in Stratford, where she could easily have met William. But that's not known for sure. What we do know is that Anne became pregnant in the fall of 1582, and named William as the father. Society's rules at the time required the young couple to get married.

During Shakespeare's time courtship and marriage were more like a business deal than a romantic relationship. The couple's parents often arranged the marriage between their children. The bride's dowry was a major factor, and no one cared too much if the bride and groom were in love or if they even liked each other.

But Anne and William's marriage was not likely an arranged one. Men usually didn't marry until they reached their mid-20s. At that point the man would typically have worked long enough and earned enough

William Shakespeare

A drawing is thought to be a portrait of Anne Hathaway.

AN IMAGINED LIFE

Even though we know little about William Shakespeare's life, writers have used their imaginations to write about what it could have been. The movie *Shakespeare in Love* starred actor Joseph Fiennes as a young Shakespeare trying to write one of his most famous plays, *Romeo and Juliet*. The movie won seven Academy Awards in 1999, including Best Picture. In 2015 the Broadway musical *Something Rotten!* imagined what would have happened if musical plays had been around to compete with Shakespeare's famous works.

William Shakespeare

money to provide for a new family. Women, however, were usually several years younger than their husbands when they married.

Therefore, 18-year-old Shakespeare's marriage to a woman eight years older was unusual for the time. Shakespeare's plays may offer some explanation. Many are about young love, so many historians believe that he and Anne must have been in love. Apart from the age difference, Anne would have been considered a good match for William. She was from the same social class and brought a suitable dowry to the marriage.

There's no record of the date of William and Anne's wedding, but it probably occurred within days after the marriage license was issued. The church season of Advent was about to start, and churches generally didn't perform marriages then. William and Anne's daughter, Susanna, was born five months later and was baptized May 26, 1583.

Little is known about William and Anne's early married life. They may have lived with his parents on

Henley Street. Shakespeare's mother might have helped Anne with baby Susanna.

In the winter of 1585 Anne had twins, a boy and a girl. They were baptized February 2, and named Hamnet and Judith, after the Shakespeares' friends Hamnet and Judith Sadler. When the Sadlers had their own son, they named him William in return.

After the twins' baptism, there's again no official record of Shakespeare's life until 1592, when he was first mentioned as a London playwright. Historians call the seven years "the lost years." Various ideas exist about what he was doing at that time.

As a married man with three children, Shakespeare would have had to work to support his family. Perhaps he worked for his father in the glove shop. Because some of his plays reflect a great deal of knowledge about horses, he may have cared for the horses of noble people who visited Stratford. Some even suggest that he may have traveled to Italy during this time, since several of his plays are set there.

William Shakespeare

Traveling acting companies often performed in the yard outside taverns.

One popular idea about Shakespeare's lost years concerns a traveling acting company that visited Stratford in 1587. The company was called the Queen's Men, because Queen Elizabeth I was its patron. One of its actors had been killed in a bar fight, so the company was short one actor when it arrived in

Inspiring Stories

ACTING COMPANIES

Acting companies were made up of actors, playwrights, directors, and costume makers. Most companies had 10 to 12 members, all of whom were men. It wasn't considered appropriate for women to appear on stage. Boys or young men played women's roles.

During Shakespeare's time most people didn't travel far from where they lived. Roads weren't well maintained, and only wealthy people could afford horse-drawn wagons and carriages. So theater companies traveled to their audiences. They loaded costumes, makeup, and props in wagons and rode around the countryside. They staged shows outdoors, at fairs, in taverns, and in the large manor houses owned by members of the upper class. As they traveled, a few members would ride on ahead to a town and ask the mayor for permission to perform there.

Acting companies needed a patron—a wealthy nobleman or even a member of royalty who gave them money and supplied them with places to perform. When acting companies came to manor houses to perform, everyone who lived in the great house—family, friends, and even servants—gathered to watch the play. It was one of the few forms of entertainment in their work-filled lives.

The plays were exciting, and the actors were the celebrities of their day. People were interested in how they spoke, dressed, and behaved.

William Shakespeare

Stratford. Shakespeare might have stepped in to help. And if he didn't join the Queen's Men, he might have joined another acting company.

William's name appears with those of his parents in a Stratford lawsuit in 1588. But Shakespeare may not have been living in Stratford anymore. Whether he left with an acting company or on his own, historians believe that some time during the "lost years" Shakespeare left Stratford, possibly in 1587. He left his wife and children behind to go to London, the center of theater life.

London was a bustling port on the Thames River.

Chapter Five
EARLY SUCCESS IN LONDON

London during Shakespeare's time was a busy, crowded city populated by almost 200,000 people. London was England's capital city and the home of Queen Elizabeth I and her court. It was also one of the world's chief trading and commercial centers. People from all over England traveled to London to seek their fortunes.

London had three main theaters—the Swan, the Rose, and Burbage's. Shakespeare may have found work at one or more of the theaters. Each theater had a resident acting company. A small group of owners ran both the theater and company. The owners were usually the company's leading actors. But theater companies also had other jobs to fill, such as people to tend the horses of audience members. Other employees called prompters waited just offstage and whispered cues to actors who forgot their lines. A prompter, like an understudy, sometimes took the place of an actor who was sick. Some were even promoted to actors. Young boys served as apprentices. They ran errands, carried costumes, and moved scenery.

Acting was hard work. The actors put on a different play each day, six days a week, learning about 800 lines for each play. Boys between the ages of 10 and 15 whose voices hadn't changed played the parts of women.

At first Shakespeare probably played minor parts, but eventually he took on leading roles and began writing plays for the company. He was definitely a playwright by 1592. That year another playwright, Robert Greene, published a pamphlet that criticized his writing and acting. Greene called Shakespeare "Shake-scene" because of his thundering voice and his

ELIZABETHAN THEATERS

Theaters of Shakespeare's time were not like those of today. There were some elegant private theaters for people of the upper class, but most theaters were public theaters. They had no artificial lighting, so plays could be performed only during the day, usually in the afternoon. Public theaters were also built around a courtyard that had no roof, so plays were performed only in the warmer months.

At one end of the courtyard was a stage, which projected into the courtyard. On the other end and continuing along the sides were three levels of seats called galleries. The regular admission fee of one penny allowed an attendee to stand and watch.

Wealthier audience members could pay extra to sit in the galleries. The stage had a main level in front and an upper level at the back. A small partial roof, usually made of straw, covered the upper stage and some of the main stage. The stage floor often had a trap door, which actors used to disappear from the stage or appear to rise into the air.

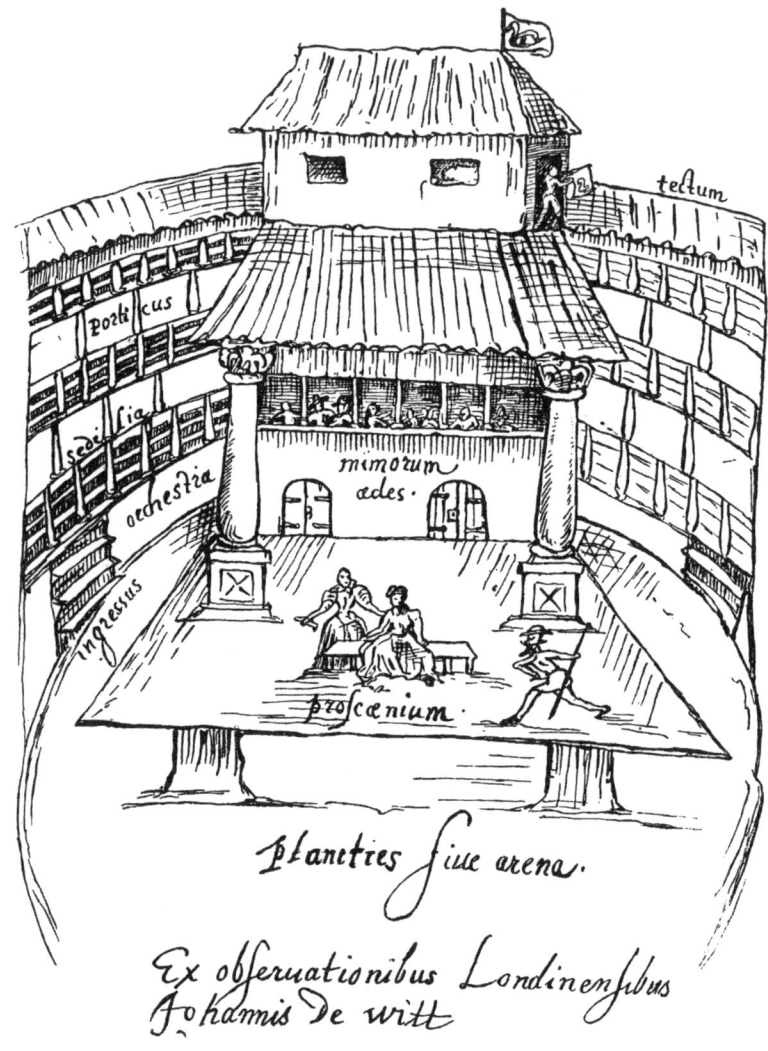

A typical Elizabethan theater had a stage, galleries, and courtyard.

dramatic writing. Greene also accused Shakespeare of stealing material from other playwrights and scolded him for believing that he could write as well as a university-educated playwright. At the time Greene was a well-known author of plays, poems, and novels. He had graduated from Cambridge University and may have been jealous that Shakespeare was doing so well with much less education.

During his career Shakespeare wrote three types of plays—histories, comedies, and tragedies. He generally concentrated on one type of play at a time.

Early in his career, historical plays were very popular, and Shakespeare wrote a number of them. He based most of their storylines on works by English historians and Roman authors, while adding his own language, wit, and humor. This was a big change, since most historical plays of the time had dull plots and wooden, one-dimensional characters. Events in the kings' and queens' lives were blamed on destiny, which made the characters powerless and cut down on the action.

Shakespeare took a different approach. He wrote the historical characters as real-life people with both weaknesses and strengths. He showed how their faults and feelings influenced their decisions and changed

Inspiring Stories

the course of history. In doing so he made them more appealing to his audiences and increased the popularity of his work.

Shakespeare's first history plays were a series of three plays about England's King Henry VI. The plays tell the story of the king's reign, including bloody wars, violence, and murder. Ned Allyn, the leading actor of the time, played King Henry. Years later Shakespeare wrote additional "Henry Plays," as they are often called—two about Henry IV, one about Henry V, and one about Henry VIII. Other plays from this period include the comedies *The Comedy of Errors*, *The Taming of the Shrew*, and *Two Gentlemen of Verona*, and the histories *Richard III* and *King John*.

Unlike most playwrights of the time, Shakespeare wrote only for his own acting company. As he wrote, he kept the theater's structure and his actors' abilities in mind, tailoring the scenes, plots, and characters to their strengths.

Shakespeare had written from five to seven plays by 1592. But since he didn't keep a record, it's unknown

William Shakespeare

STAGES OF SHAKESPEARE'S CAREER

Shakespeare's career can be divided roughly into four stages, during which he often concentrated on a specific type of play.

Stage 1, 1590-1594: History plays and light comedies, including *Henry VI* (parts I, II, III), *Richard III*, *The Comedy of Errors*, and *The Taming of the Shrew*

Stage 2, 1595-1600: Comedies such as *A Midsummer Night's Dream*, *The Merchant of Venice*, *Much Ado About Nothing*, and *Twelfth Night*, as well as the tragedies *Romeo and Juliet* and *Julius Caesar*

Stage 3, 1601-1608: The great tragedies, including *Hamlet*, *Othello*, *King Lear*, and *Macbeth*

Stage 4, 1609-1613: Plays with a sense of calm and peacefulness, such as *The Winter's Tale*, *The Tempest*, and *Cymbeline*

exactly when each was written. He also didn't publish his plays. Few playwrights did at that time, because they weren't considered serious writers. Serious writers wrote books and poetry.

Each time a play was performed, it could be slightly different. Actors didn't memorize their lines word for word—they often improvised them. More than knowing their exact lines, playwrights and directors wanted actors to remember when to enter and exit the stage.

Although a number of Shakespeare's plays were printed during his lifetime, he had little to do with their publication. The printing press was very new and publishing was still difficult and expensive, especially because of the high cost of paper. Shakespeare's actors also didn't want him to publish his work. They were worried that if the plays were published, other acting companies would perform them, cutting into the company's business. As Shakespeare's fame increased, this became even more important.

But by 1592 everything in London had changed with the rise of the bubonic plague. Although Shakespeare's

William Shakespeare

ACTING ADVANTAGE

Shakespeare may have lost his hair at a fairly young age. This gave him an unusual advantage as an actor because it allowed him to play the parts of older men.

Inspiring Stories

Shakespeare read his plays to his family when they gathered together.

increased wealth and better living conditions reduced his chances of getting sick, he was fast losing his audience. At times about 1,000 people died each week. Healthy people were fleeing the city. Because large gatherings exposed more people to the plague, performances in theaters were outlawed.

William Shakespeare

With the theaters closed, Shakespeare had to find another way to earn a living. He decided to stay in London and continue writing. But writing plays wouldn't earn him any money. He decided to try his hand at another type of writing—poetry.

Shakespeare read his works to Queen Elizabeth I and her court.

A PUBLISHED POET

With the theaters closed, Shakespeare found another way to share his stories. He wrote two long poems, called narratives. Unlike his plays, the poems were published. *Venus and Adonis* was published in 1593, and *The Rape of Lucrece* was published in 1594. The narratives were both based on the ancient Roman writer Ovid's tales—*Venus and Adonis* on the *Metamorphoses* and *The Rape of Lucrece* on the *Fasti*. They weren't published in the format that books of today are, though. The poems were published as quartos, which were printed sheets of paper folded into quarters and sold unbound. If people wanted their books to have covers, they had to make them.

In Shakespeare's day poets often dedicated their poems to another person. The person was almost always a noble, such as a lord or a prince, who could become a patron to the poet. Sometimes the nobles hired poets to write for them, and sometimes poets just dedicated their work to nobles, hoping they'd like the poems and then pay for them. Shakespeare dedicated both *Venus and Adonis* and *The Rape of Lucrece* to 19-year-old Henry Wriothesley, the Earl of Southampton.

In his dedication of *Venus and Adonis*, Shakespeare wrote: "I know not how I shall offend in dedicating my unpolished lines to your lordship, nor how the world will censure me for choosing so strong a prop to support so weak a burden only, if your honour seem but pleased, I account myself highly praised, and vow to take advantage of all idle hours, till I have honoured you with some graver labour."

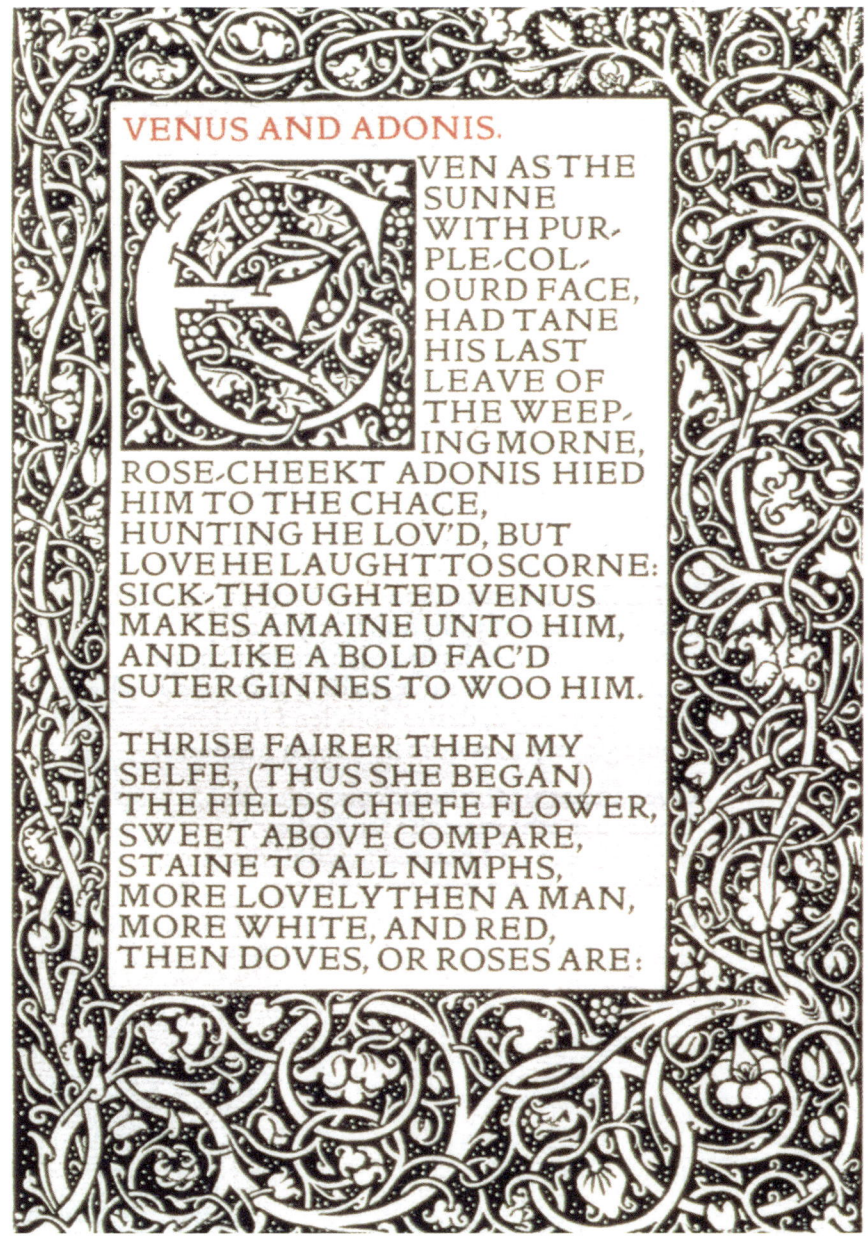

A woodcut of the opening of Shakespeare's 1593 narrative poem, Venus and Adonis

By calling his work "unpolished lines," Shakespeare let the earl know that he was modest about his own work. He also offered to provide the earl with more poetry if the earl was pleased with what he read. In fact, Shakespeare wanted to become the earl's personal poet. Offering to "take advantage of all idle hours" is Shakespeare's way of saying that he would write tirelessly to please the earl.

LIFE WITH THE RICH AND FAMOUS

Some historians believe that Shakespeare may have met the Earl of Southampton before he became a successful playwright. Soon after he moved to London, Shakespeare may have tended the horses of nobles who were attending plays and earned their trust. Shakespeare very well may have used the relationships to help him in his career as a playwright and poet. Shakespeare's clever handling of rich, noble people served him well throughout his life. In later years he became a favorite of kings and queens, which helped expand his fame and wealth.

Henry Wriothesley, the Earl of Southampton

The plea may have worked. Some historians believe Shakespeare received money from the earl that he later used to invest in a theater company. Shakespeare's dedication of *The Rape of Lucrece* is flattering and affectionate, which suggests great gratitude on Shakespeare's part. It included the lines: "What I have done is yours; what I have to do is yours; being part in all I have, devoted yours."

Shakespeare also wrote shorter poems called sonnets. A sonnet has 14 lines and a specific rhyming pattern in which certain lines must rhyme with other lines. Shakespeare's sonnets were often written in the pattern ABAB CDCD EFEF GG. Each letter stands for a line that ends in a particular sound—A lines rhyme with other A lines, B lines with other B lines, C with C, etc.

Sonnets are also written in iambic pentameter. The word iambic refers to the placement of the accented syllables. In poetry that follows an iambic pattern, every other syllable is stressed, beginning with an unaccented syllable. Pentameter refers to the five iambic groupings that make up a line.

Shakespeare wrote 154 sonnets. The first 126 sonnets are addressed to the same person, a rich nobleman whom he calls "Fair Youth." Some historians believe that the nobleman was the Earl of Southampton, but

SHAKE-SPEARES

SONNETS.

Neuer before Imprinted.

AT LONDON
By G. Eld for T. T. and are
to be folde by John Wright, dwelling
at Chrift Church gate.
1609.

The title page of the first printing of Shakespeare's sonnets stressed their newness.

Inspiring Stories

EXPANDING THE LANGUAGE

In his poems and plays, Shakespeare invented many new words and expressions, many of which are still used. They include the words bandit, moonbeam, mimic, luggage, and leapfrog, as well as the expressions for goodness' sake, a sorry sight, in my mind's eye, and eaten out of house and home.

others doubt it, since some of the poems show the nobleman in an unflattering light. The first 12 sonnets try to convince the young nobleman to marry and have children. Some Shakespeare historians think that the nobleman's mother may have asked Shakespeare to write the poems.

The last 28 sonnets are written to women. They are called the Dark Lady poems because many of them describe a beautiful woman with "raven black" hair and eyes. Shakespeare refers to the woman as his mistress and indicates that she is married. She may have been a married woman with whom he had a relationship. However, at the time the word mistress didn't necessarily mean something romantic. Sometimes it simply referred to a woman. And at least one of the poems, Sonnet 145, appears to be written about his wife, Anne.

Shakespeare's sonnets were published in 1609, although probably not by him. He thought of the poems as private and probably never intended to print them.

Shakespeare was a successful writer, actor, and acting company owner.

Chapter Seven
SUCCESS AS A PLAYWRIGHT

Although Shakespeare is known today for his plays, they weren't what made him rich. Shakespeare made most of his money by being a partner in an acting company with Richard Burbage and William Kempe. When the plague scare ended in 1594 and the theaters reopened, the company returned to the stage with a new name, the Lord Chamberlain's Men. In addition to his duties as an owner and actor, Shakespeare wrote an average of two plays a year for the

Inspiring Stories

Shakespeare's acting troupe was often invited to perform before the queen and her court.

company. Queen Elizabeth was a major supporter of the company, and Shakespeare and his partners were becoming famous and wealthy.

Shakespeare concentrated on history plays and comedies from 1594 to 1600. Plays from the period include the comedies *A Midsummer Night's Dream, Love's Labours Lost, The Merchant of Venice, As You Like It, Much Ado About Nothing, Twelfth Night,* and *The Merry Wives of*

ROMEO AND JULIET

Possibly the most famous love story of all time, Shakespeare's tragedy *Romeo and Juliet* is one of his most frequently staged plays. The play, which Shakespeare based on an Italian narrative poem, takes place in Verona, Italy. Teenagers Romeo Montague and Juliet Capulet fall in love, despite the longstanding feud between their parents. They secretly marry, but misunderstandings cause them both to commit suicide, after which their families sadly end their feud. The play has been made into several movies. Its plot was also used in the famous Broadway musical *West Side Story* and the 2006 TV movie *High School Musical*.

Some historians believe Shakespeare may have taken some inspiration for *Romeo and Juliet* from his own life. They think some bad feelings might have existed between his family and the Hathaways around the time of Anne and William's marriage.

Windsor; the histories *Richard II, Henry IV,* and *Henry V*; and the tragedies *Romeo and Juliet* and *Julius Caesar.*

In 1596 Shakespeare applied to the same College of Arms that had rejected his father's application. This time the college awarded the family a coat of arms. At the time John Shakespeare was still alive, and William may have wanted the coat of arms because he knew it was important to his father. The yellow, black, and red emblem featured the French words "Non sans droit," which mean "Not without right." William may have chosen the motto as a comment on the College of Arms' previous refusal of his family's application.

Now Shakespeare had a coat of arms he could pass on to his son, Hamnet. But tragically, Hamnet died August 11, 1596. He was only 11 years old. No records exist of what caused Hamnet's death—if it was an illness such as the plague or if the boy died in an accident. Shakespeare wrote many of his tragic plays after his son's death, including *Hamlet*, in which he played the role of the ghost of Hamlet's father.

William Shakespeare

Hamlet encounters the ghost of his father in Shakespeare's famous play.

Historians believe he used this role to express his grief over his son's death.

By 1597 the Lord Chamberlain's Men needed a new theater. The company owned the theater building, but they rented the land it was built on. Their landlord kept raising the rent, and once the lease expired, he kicked

Richard Burbage was one of the leading actors of the Lord Chamberlain's Men.

them out. The company temporarily moved to another theater, the Curtain.

Richard Burbage and his brother Cuthbert convinced Shakespeare and three other actors in the company to contribute money for a new theater in

FRIENDS AND RIVALS

Shakespeare wasn't the only well-regarded playwright of his time. Ben Jonson, Christopher Marlowe, Thomas Kyd, and Robert Greene were all successful playwrights in London who were around Shakespeare's age. All were well educated and achieved some success before the London theaters closed because of the bubonic plague in 1592. Robert Greene died four days before the theaters closed, just after publishing his pamphlet that criticized Shakespeare. Marlowe was killed during a fight with another man in 1593. Kyd died the next year.

By the time the theaters reopened in 1594, only Shakespeare and Jonson were left. The two men were friends and competitors for the rest of Shakespeare's life. Shakespeare may have even acted in some of Jonson's plays with his acting company. Jonson died at age 65 in 1637, leaving behind a collection of poems and mostly comic plays.

Inspiring Stories

exchange for a share of ownership in late 1598. They pooled their money and rented a site in the London suburb of Southwark. One night Shakespeare and the other company members took apart their building, board by board, and ferried it across the Thames River to the new site, where they rebuilt it. They called the rebuilt theater the Globe, probably because of its round shape. Like most theaters of its time, it was built around a roofless courtyard.

PERFECT FIRST DRAFT

Shakespeare had a reputation for never changing lines once he wrote them down. It may have been because of the high cost of paper at the time. The paper required to write one play would have cost Shakespeare all the money he could earn in a month. He probably used a quill pen made of a large bird feather to write on the paper.

William Shakespeare

Theatergoers flocked to performances at the Globe.

The Globe opened in May 1599 and held 2,500 to 3,000 people. Probably the first play at the Globe was *Henry V.* A line in its opening speech referred to "this wooden O," meaning the shape of the theater.

Inspiring Stories

The Globe was the finest theater of its day.

Atop the theater was a flag with the theater's crest—the Greek god Hercules holding a globe on his shoulders. Depending on the play being performed, other flags may have been raised. Sometimes the flag showed an image from the play. Other times color-coded flags told the audience what to expect. A black flag meant the company would be performing a tragedy, a white flag meant comedy, and a red flag meant a history play.

Above the entrance doors was a Latin phrase from one of Shakespeare's plays, *Totus mundus agit histrionem*, "The whole world's a theater." Shakespeare liked the line and wrote an expanded version of it in his play *As You Like It*:

"All the world's a stage,

And all the men and women merely players:

They have their exits and their entrances;

And one man in his time plays many parts."

Even though the new location meant that most theatergoers had to take a boat across the Thames, the theater quickly became a success. Owning the theater building and controlling the land gave the Lord Chamberlain's Men an important edge over their competitors—they were able to make more money off of their productions than other companies were.

A scene from Hamlet, *one of Shakespeare's most well-regarded plays*

Chapter Eight
ACHIEVING FAME

With the opening of the Globe, Shakespeare was even more productive as a playwright. He wrote his greatest tragedies from 1601 to 1608—*Hamlet, King Lear, Othello, Antony and Cleopatra,* and *Macbeth.* The plays are among Shakespeare's best, written at the peak of his talent and the height of his career. But all of his plays weren't tragic and gloomy. During this time he also wrote and produced the comedies *All's Well That Ends Well* and *Measure for Measure.*

Shakespeare continued to write his plays with his fellow actors in mind. Many of his comedies

Will Kempe (right) was a famous dancer and actor.

were written to suit the company's best comic actor, Will Kempe. Tragedies were written to suit Richard Burbage, the company's leading tragic actor.

In February 1603 Queen Elizabeth I died at age 69. Her cousin James became King James I. James was also a fan of the company and its plays, and he became its new patron. He offered the company a royal license,

William Shakespeare

which allowed them to call themselves the King's Men. With their name change, they received cloth to make special uniforms called livery. The company also regularly entertained the king at court. The King's Men became London's leading theatrical group. Shakespeare created some of his most important work during this time.

The King's Men leased an indoor theater called Blackfriars in 1608. It was part of a former monastery near the Thames River. Blackfriars had a full roof, artificial lighting, and was probably heated as well. Now the company could present plays during the winter as well as summer. Blackfriars was smaller than the Globe, seating 700 people, but the more comfortable conditions allowed Shakespeare and his partners to charge an admission price twice that of the Globe.

Shakespeare wrote four plays from 1609 to 1613, the last of his career. The final plays are *Cymbeline*, *The Winter's Tale*, *The Tempest*, and *Henry VIII*. Historians believe that he may have written the history play *Henry VIII* with John Fletcher, who was part of the

Inspiring Stories

King James I was a patron of the arts.

King's Men. Shakespeare also is believed to have contributed to another play, *The Two Noble Kinsmen*, but Fletcher did most of the writing. In his late 40s,

TREASONOUS PLOT

Shakespeare referred to current events in his plays, but he wasn't involved in politics. He was, however, unknowingly involved in a plot to overthrow his patron, Queen Elizabeth I.

Robert Devereux, the Earl of Essex, had fallen out of favor with the queen and led a group of people who wanted Elizabeth overthrown in 1601. The group included Shakespeare's former patron, the Earl of Southampton. Essex sent Sir Gilly Meyrick to ask the Lord Chamberlain's Men to perform *Richard II* on February 7 at the Globe. In the play King Richard breaks his own laws and is overthrown by his cousin. Essex and Meyrick hoped the play would inspire others to join their cause.

Shakespeare's troupe performed the play, but the overthrow attempt failed. The Earl of Essex, Meyrick, and the Earl of Southampton were all tried and convicted of treason. Southampton was later freed, but Essex, Meyrick, and four other men were executed. The acting company faced no punishment. In fact, the queen asked them to perform *Richard II* at her palace on February 24—the night before the earl's beheading.

Inspiring Stories

Shakespeare set his plays in locations throughout Europe and North Africa.

approaching what was old age at the time, Shakespeare seemed to be winding down and preparing for a new chapter in his life.

William Shakespeare

THE TEMPEST

Most historians agree that only a small part of Shakespeare's work was autobiographical. Shakespeare wrote more about people in his life than he did about himself.

But *The Tempest*, one of his final plays, may have been written about the issues he was facing in his own life. The play's main character, Prospero, has magical powers that he uses to correct a series of wrongs and set people on the proper course for their lives. At the end of the play, Prospero gives up his magical abilities, saying, "Let your indulgence set me free."

Many historians believe that Shakespeare used the character of Prospero to tell his audience that he was ready to retire from playwriting.

Inspiring Stories

The gardens at New Place in Stratford

Shakespeare had lived in London for more than 20 years. His wife and children had never joined him there, although he visited them from time to time. In 1597 he had bought a large brick house in Stratford called New Place, where Anne, Susanna, and Judith lived comfortably. Five years later he bought an estate

William Shakespeare

near Stratford that included a farmhouse and 107 acres (43 hectares) of land.

The Shakespeare family experienced several changes in the early years of the new century. By 1608 both of Shakespeare's parents had died. His daughter Susanna married Dr. John Hall in 1607, and the next year she gave birth to Shakespeare's first grandchild, a girl named Elizabeth. Shakespeare may have been lonely for his family or just wishing for a change from London. In any case, around 1611, Shakespeare left London and went home to Stratford for good. He was 47 years old.

Shakespeare moved into New Place with Anne and became part of village life. He didn't write plays, because Stratford had banned them as being evil, and the village had no theater or acting company. Shakespeare kept his half-pint mug at the local tavern where he drank every Saturday afternoon. He saw his daughters and granddaughter often. It may have been one of the happiest and contented periods of his life.

Shakespeare's fame lives on more than 400 years after his death.

Chapter Nine
LATER YEARS

Shakespeare's daughter Judith married Thomas Quiney, a wine merchant who was the son of a neighbor in Stratford, on February 10, 1616. At the wedding reception, some people said Shakespeare drank too much and caught a fever that eventually killed him. But many Shakespeare experts don't believe the story, saying instead that he just became sicker as he got older.

Six weeks after Judith's wedding, Shakespeare revised his will. He may have been concerned about Judith's situation. Shortly after her marriage, it was revealed that her husband had fathered a child with another woman. Also, the marriage took place during the religious season of Lent, and Thomas hadn't paid the extra fee for a marriage license that would allow them to marry then. The actions caused Thomas to be fined and also excommunicated from the church.

In his will, Shakespeare left household items and homes to his daughters, along with items to his granddaughter, sister, and nephews. His signature looks a bit shaky, as though he were weak or sick. His only mention of his wife is that she should receive his "second-best bed." Was that an insult? Maybe not. Some historians say that the "best bed" was reserved for guests, and the homeowners slept in the second-best bed. Other historians think that Shakespeare was sleeping in the best bed during his illness, and he didn't want to leave Anne his sickbed. But no one knows for sure.

Shakespeare's will didn't mention his most important possessions—his poems and plays. At the time neither he nor anyone else could have imagined that people

William Shakespeare

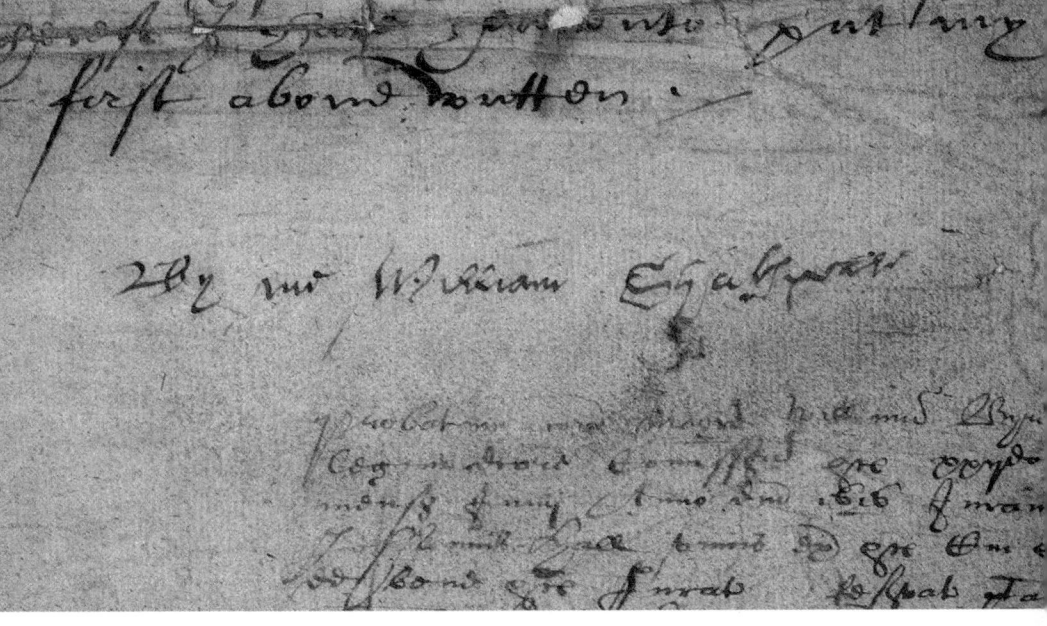

Shakespeare's shaky signature on his will suggests he might have been in poor health.

would still be reading and performing his plays hundreds of years later.

Shakespeare died at New Place on April 23, 1616, the day believed to be his 52nd birthday. He was buried in a tomb in Holy Trinity Church in Stratford, where he had been baptized. The epitaph on his gravestone reads:

> "Good friend for Jesus sake forbeare, To dig the dust enclosed here. Blessed be the man that spares these stones, and cursed be he that moves my bones."

Inspiring Stories

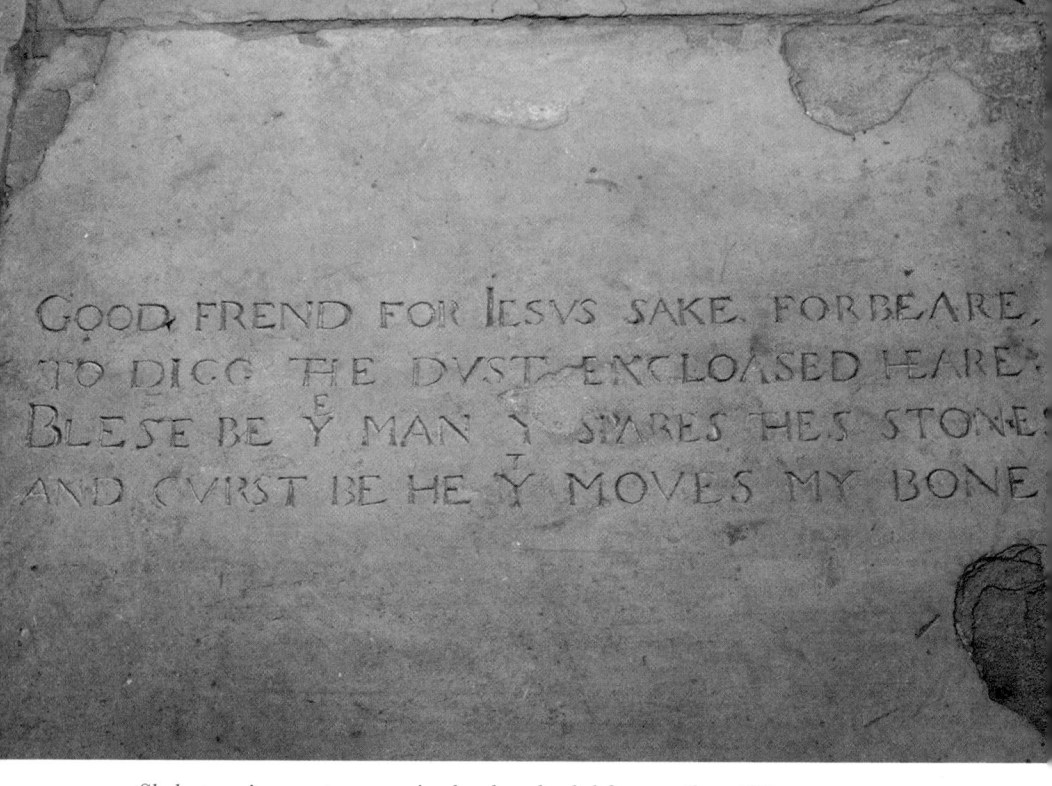

Shakespeare's gravestone warning has been heeded for more than 400 years.

At the time old graves sometimes were dug up to make room for new graves. Shakespeare may have written the epitaph to make sure that no one would ever disturb his grave. To this day, no one has.

Stonemason Gheeraert Janssen the Younger carved a bust of Shakespeare. It was painted and placed on Shakespeare's tomb in the church.

Anne lived seven more years after William's death. She died August 6, 1623, at age 67, and was buried in Holy Trinity next to her husband. Shakespeare's oldest daughter, Susanna Hall, died in 1649 at age 66. His younger daughter, Judith Quiney, died in 1662 at age 77.

SHAKESPEARE'S DESCENDANTS

William Shakespeare left no direct descendants. His daughter Susanna had just one child, Elizabeth Hall. Although Elizabeth married twice, she died childless at age 61. Shakespeare's younger daughter, Judith, had three sons, all born after her father's death. Her oldest son, Shakespeare Quiney, died as a baby. Judith's other two sons died as young men, leaving no children. William Shakespeare's brothers were also childless, but his sister, Joan Shakespeare Hall, had four children. Her descendants are the only living connection to Shakespeare's immediate family.

Inspiring Stories

The fame Shakespeare achieved after his death has helped his name live on. When Shakespeare died, members of his acting company decided to gather his works and publish them. Two members, John Heminges and Henry Condell, went through the actors' scripts and pieced together versions of the plays. It took them about seven years.

They published *Mr. William Shakespeare's Comedies, Histories, and Tragedies* on November 8, 1623. The publication included 36 plays and was called the *First Folio of 1623*. A folio isn't quite a book. Like the earlier quartos, the folio was folded paper with no cover, although some did have a calfskin binding. Shakespeare's good friend Ben Jonson, another important writer and playwright of the time, wrote a heartfelt introduction. The *First Folio* sold for one British pound. About 250 copies of the *First Folio* still exist. Each is worth more than $2 million.

The first printing of the *First Folio* sold out, and the book was reprinted several more times. Later editions include Shakespeare's poems and sonnets. The printed

William Shakespeare

Ben Jonson wrote the introduction to the First Folio *of 1623.*

plays made it easier for other acting companies to perform Shakespeare, and his fame spread. More copies of his plays were published, and more people read Shakespeare and quoted his lines. As the centuries passed, Shakespeare's works were added to literature textbooks all over the world. Even today most students

Inspiring Stories

A scene from Shakespeare's comedy The Taming of the Shrew

read at least one of Shakespeare's plays sometime during their education. There are still repertory companies that perform only Shakespeare's work. Some even perform it outside, as Shakespeare's acting companies did. These performances are often called Shakespeare in the Park.

THE GLOBE THEATER

Even though he had moved from London, Shakespeare still owned part of the theater company. Two years after he left London, on June 29, 1613, disaster struck the Globe. During a performance of *Henry VIII*, a cannon used as a prop shot sparks on the theater's straw half-roof. Within an hour the theater burned to the ground. The company built a new theater with a tiled roof on the site.

The new Globe Theatre operated until 1642. At that time a large religious group called the Puritans blamed diseases such as the plague on the English people's sinful behavior. Attending plays was among the things the Puritans considered sinful. They pressured Parliament, which made the laws of the country, to close all theaters, which it did. The Globe was torn down in 1644. Apartments were built on its site.

The Puritans' power had decreased by 1660 and theaters opened again, but not the Globe. More than 300 years later, in 1993, construction began on a new Globe Theater near the site of the original. It was built according to what is known about the original theater. Queen Elizabeth II dedicated the theater when it opened in May 1997 with a production of *Henry V*.

Inspiring Stories

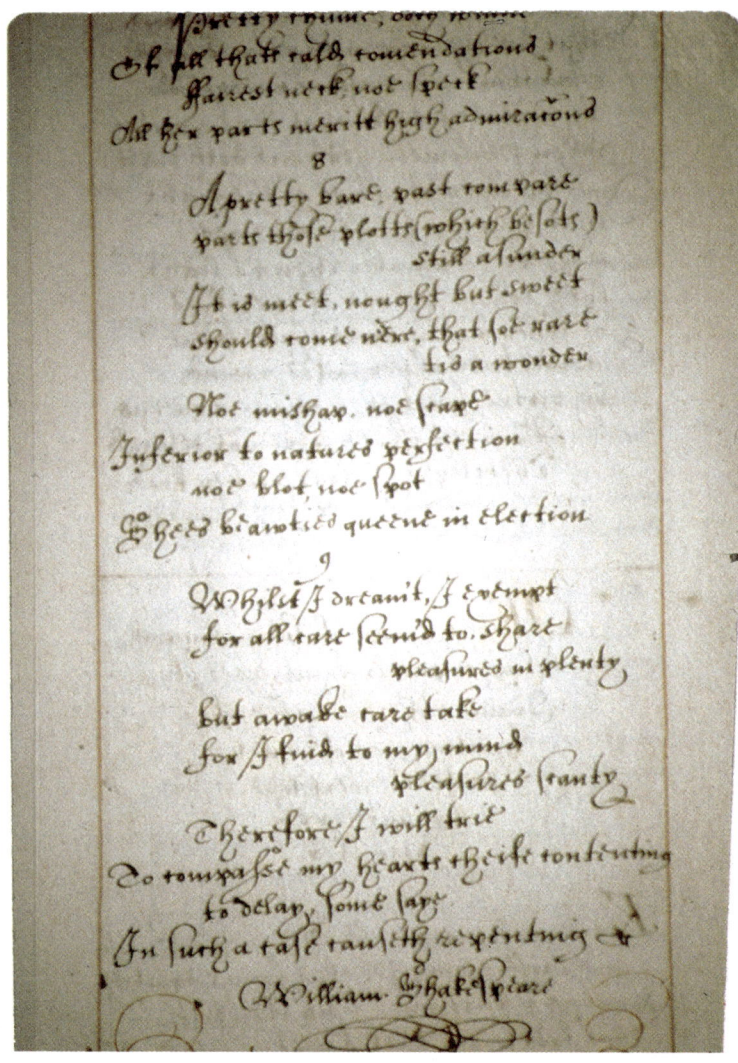

A recently discovered poem is written in Shakespeare's handwriting.

Any list of the greatest books ever written includes the complete works of William Shakespeare. His plays have been filmed as movies and choreographed

AUTHORSHIP CONTROVERSY

Over the years some people have doubted that one man, especially one with a limited education, could write so many masterpieces by himself. Some even question whether Shakespeare wrote any plays at all.

How printers worked at the time adds to the confusion. They often published works without the author's permission or published them under another author's name. Shakespeare was a common name at the time, and some historians wonder if an educated nobleman or another writer such as Ben Jonson or Christopher Marlowe might have used "Shakespeare" as a false name for some of their work. Or perhaps they collaborated with Shakespeare, contributing ideas or taking turns writing parts.

Historians have also suggested a number of other possible authors for the works, even Queen Elizabeth I. Others suggest that the author may have been Francis Bacon, a great scholar of the Elizabethan era.

But when Shakespeare's plays became famous, no other author stepped forward to claim credit, even after his death. Today few Shakespeare experts doubt that anyone but Shakespeare himself is responsible for his amazing body of work.

for the ballet. And with the many new words and expressions he invented, Shakespeare forever changed the English language.

Teenagers today can watch *Romeo and Juliet* and know that a writer living 400 years ago understood their feelings. Adults can watch *King Lear* and know that Shakespeare understood the frustration of trying to help an aging parent. Audiences hear Hamlet grieve for his dead father in *Hamlet* or hear Petruchio tease Kate in *The Taming of the Shrew*, and feel they are in the company of friends.

Even today people can learn important lessons from his work. As his friend Ben Jonson said, "He was not of an age but for all time!"

William Shakespeare

A statue of William Shakespeare sits in the village of Stratford, the birthplace and burial site of the English playwright and poet.

Timeline

1585
Twins Judith and Hamnet are born

1583
Daughter Susanna is born

1564
Born on or around April 23; baptized April 26 at Holy Trinity Church in Stratford, England

1582
Marries Anne Hathaway

1594
Publishes narrative poem, *The Rape of Lucrece*

1585–1592
Known as the lost years; possibly left Stratford in 1587 to join a traveling acting company

1596
Applies for and receives a coat of arms; son Hamnet dies

1593
Publishes first narrative poem, *Venus and Adonis*

Timeline

1609
Sonnets are published

SHAKE-SPEARES
SONNETS.
Neuer before Imprinted.

AT LONDON
By G. Eld for T. T. and are
to be solde by John Wright, dwelling
at Christ Church gate.
1609.

1599
Globe Theatre opens

1608
Blackfriars Theatre opens

1613
Globe Theater burns and is rebuilt

1611
Returns to Stratford after more than 20 years in London

1616
Dies April 23 at age 52

Glossary

bail—sum of money paid to a court to allow someone accused of a crime to be set free until his or her trial

catechism—religious instruction that is often conducted in the form of questions and answers

choreograph—to create and arrange dance movements

contagious—spreadable, as in disease

courtship—the process of seeking to win a promise of marriage

destiny—predetermined course of events

epitaph—words written in memory of a dead person, especially on a gravestone

excommunicate—to exclude from taking part in the church

irony—state of affairs or an event that seems deliberately contrary to what one expects

livery—special uniform

patron—someone who supports a writer or artist

playwright—person who writes plays

psalm—sacred song or hymn, in particular those contained in the biblical Book of Psalms and used in Christian and Jewish worship

repertory—the repeated performance of several plays one after the other by one company of actors

rhetoric—the art of speaking and writing effectively, especially as a way to persuade or influence people

surety—person who agrees to take legal responsibility for someone else's debts or obligations

tutor—teacher who gives lessons to just one student or a small group of students

vaccine—medicine that prevents a disease

Further Reading

Chrisp, Peter. *Eyewitness Shakespeare.*
New York: DK Publishing, 2015.

Griffiths, Katie. *Romeo and Juliet.*
New York: Cavendish Square Publishing, 2016.

Robson, David. *Shakespeare's Globe Theater.*
San Diego: ReferencePoint Press, 2014.

Shuter, Paul. *William Shakespeare: A Man for All Times.*
Chicago: Capstone Heinemann Library, 2014.

Internet Sites

Use FactHound to find Internet sites related to this book. All of the sites on FactHound have been researched by our staff.

Here's all you do:

Visit www.facthound.com

Type in this code: 9780756551636

Other Books In This Series

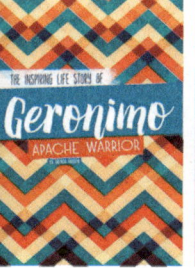   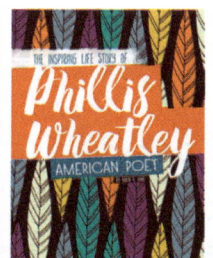 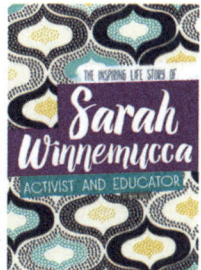

Source Notes

Page 12, line 6: William Shakespeare. *As You Like It*. Act II, scene 7. Shakespeare Online. 27 April 2016. http://www.shakespeare-online.com/plays/asu_2_7.html

Page 30, line 20: William Shakespeare. *Hamlet*. Act I, scene 3. Shakespeare Online. 27 April 2016. http://www.shakespeare-online.com/plays/hamlet_1_3.html

Page 46, line 21: Anthony Holden. *William Shakespeare: The Man Behind the Genius: A Biography*. Boston: Little, Brown and Company, 1999, p. 107.

Page 58, line 15: William Shakespeare. *Venus and Adonis*. Dedication. Shakespeare Online. 27 April 2016. http://www.shakespeare-online.com/sonnets/venus.html

Page 62, line 2: William Shakespeare. *The Rape of Lucrece*. Dedication. Shakespeare Online. 27 April 2016. http://www.shakespeare-online.com/sonnets/lucrece.html

Page 75, line 3: William Shakespeare. *Henry V*. Prologue. Shakespeare Online. 27 April 2016. http://www.shakespeare-online.com/plays/henryv_1_1.html

Page 77, line 8: *As You Like It*. Act II, scene 7.

Page 85, line 10: William Shakespeare. *The Tempest*. Epilogue. Shakespeare Online. 27 April 2016. http://www.shakespeare-online.com/plays/temp_5_1.html

Page 90, line 11: Joyce Rogers. *The Second Best Bed: Shakespeare's Will in a New Light.* Westport, Conn.: Greenwood Press, 1993, pp. 74–75.

Page 91, line 8: Shakespeare's Burial. Shakespeare Online. 27 April 2016. http://www.shakespeare-online.com/biography/shakespeareburial.html

Page 100, line 13: Ben Jonson. *To the Memory of My Beloved the Author, Mr. William Shakespeare.* The Poetry Foundation. http://www.poetryfoundation.org/poem/173731

Select Bibliography

Bryson, Bill. *Shakespeare: The World as Stage.* New York: Atlas Books/HarperCollins, 2007.

Duncan-Jones, Katherine. *Ungentle Shakespeare: Scenes From His Life.* London: Arden Shakespeare, 2001.

Fraser, Russell A. *Shakespeare: The Later Years.* New York: Columbia University Press, 1992.

Gurr, Andrew. *William Shakespeare: The Extraordinary Life of the Most Successful Writer of All Time.* London: HarperCollins, 1995.

Holden, Anthony. *William Shakespeare: The Man Behind the Genius: A Biography.* Boston: Little, Brown and Company, 1999.

Krull, Kathleen. *Lives of the Writers: Comedies, Tragedies (and What the Neighbors Thought).* San Diego: Harcourt Brace, 1994.

Price, Diana. *Shakespeare's Unorthodox Biography: New Evidence of an Authorship Problem.* Westport, Conn.: Greenwood Press, 2001.

Rogers, Joyce. *The Second Best Bed: Shakespeare's Will in a New Light.* Westport, Conn.: Greenwood Press, 1993.

Rowse, A. L. *William Shakespeare: A Biography.* New York: Harper & Rowe, 1963.

Sams, Eric. *The Real Shakespeare: Retrieving the Early Years, 1564–1594.* New Haven, Conn.: Yale University Press, 1995.

Index

All's Well That Ends Well (comedy) 79
Anglican Church 28, 29
Antony and Cleopatra (tragedy) 79
Arden, Robert (grandfather) 17
As You Like It (comedy) 12, 68, 77

baptism 15, 17
Bible 28, 30
birth 15, 17, 91
bubonic plague 5–6, 7, 9, 18, 52, 54, 67, 73, 97
Burbage, Richard 67, 72, 80

childhood 20, 22, 32–33
coat of arms 20, 22, 70
Comedy of Errors, The (comedy) 50, 51
Cymbeline (comedy) 51, 81

Dark Lady poems 64–65
death 89, 91–92

education 25–26, 28, 30, 32, 49
Elizabeth I, queen of England 29, 31, 41, 45, 68, 80, 83, 99
Elizabeth II, queen of England 97
epitaph 91–92
Essex, Robert Devereux, Earl of 83

First Folio of 1623 (collection) 94

Globe Theatre 74–77, 79, 81, 83, 97
Greene, Robert 46, 48–49, 73

Hall, Elizabeth (granddaughter) 87, 90, 93
Hamlet (tragedy) 12, 30, 51, 70–71, 79, 100
Hathaway, Anne (wife) 35–36, 39–40, 43, 65, 69, 86, 87, 90, 93
Henry IV (history play) 50, 70
Henry V (history play) 50, 70, 75, 97
Henry VI (history plays) 50, 51
Henry VIII (history play) 50, 81–82, 97
High School Musical (movie) 69
Holy Trinity Church 15, 91, 92, 93

James I, king of England 80–81
Jonson, Ben 73, 94, 99, 100
Julius Caesar (tragedy) 51, 70

King John (history play) 50
King Lear (tragedy) 51, 79, 100
King's Men acting company 81–82
Kyd, Thomas 73

language 11, 26, 64, 77, 100
Life at a Glance 23
Lord Chamberlain's Men acting company 67–68, 71–72, 77, 79–80, 83
lost years 40–41, 43
Love's Labours Lost (comedy) 68

Macbeth (tragedy) 51, 79
Marlowe, Christopher 73, 99
marriage 35, 36, 39–40, 69
Measure for Measure (comedy) 79
Merchant of Venice, The (comedy) 51, 68
Merry Wives of Windsor, The (comedy) 68, 70
Metamorphoses (Ovid) 26, 57
Meyrick, Sir Gilly 83
Midsummer Night's Dream, A (comedy) 51, 68
Much Ado About Nothing (comedy) 51, 68

New Place home 86, 87, 91

Othello (tragedy) 51, 79

patrons 41, 42, 80–81, 83
publications 52, 57, 65, 94–96, 99

quartos 57–58
Queen's Men acting company 41, 43

Rape of Lucrece, The (poem) 57, 58, 60–62
Richard II (history play) 70, 83
Richard III (history play) 50, 51
Roman Catholic Church 29
Romeo and Juliet (tragedy) 12, 38, 51, 69, 70, 100
royal license 80–81

Shakespeare, Anne (sister) 18, 19
Shakespeare, Edmund (brother) 18, 93
Shakespeare, Gilbert (brother) 18, 93
Shakespeare, Hamnet (son) 12, 40, 70
Shakespeare in Love (movie) 38
Shakespeare in the Park performances 96

Index cont.

Shakespeare, Joan (sister) 16, 18, 19, 93
Shakespeare, John (father) 16, 17, 20, 29, 30, 35, 43, 70, 87
Shakespeare, Judith (daughter) 40, 86, 89, 90, 93
Shakespeare, Mary Arden (mother) 16, 17, 19, 43, 87
Shakespeare, Richard (brother) 18, 93
Shakespeare, Susanna (daughter) 39, 40, 86, 87, 90, 93
social classes 18, 20, 60
Something Rotten! (Broadway musical) 38
sonnets 62, 64–65
Southampton, Henry Wriothesley, Earl of 58, 60–62, 83

Taming of the Shrew, The (comedy) 50, 51, 100
Tempest, The (comedy) 51, 81, 85
Twelfth Night (comedy) 51, 68
Two Gentlemen of Verona (comedy) 50
Two Noble Kinsmen, The (comedy) 82

Venus and Adonis (poem) 26, 57, 58

West Side Story (Broadway musical) 69
will 89, 90
Winter's Tale, The (comedy) 51, 81

CRITICAL THINKING USING THE COMMON CORE

1. Shakespeare's plays are still popular today, more than 400 years after they were written. Why do you think they've stayed popular? Do you think any books, songs, or movies from today will be popular in 400 years? Why or why not? (Integration of Knowledge and Ideas)

2. Shakespeare had a limited education but still managed to become one of the greatest writers of all time. What qualities did he have that helped him overcome his obstacles to success? Use evidence from the text to support your answer. (Key Ideas and Details)

3. The bubonic plague killed more than half of Europe's population during the 1300s. Is there any disease today that you think could cause as much devastation? (Integration of Knowledge and Ideas)